# KIDS GET CODING

## CODING IN THE REAL WORLD

Heather Lyons

WAYLAND

# Contents

Getting started · · · · · · · · · · · 3

Everyday computers · · · · · · · · 4

Car or computer? · · · · · · · · · · 6

Road safety · · · · · · · · · · · · · · 8

Home sweet home · · · · · · · · · · 10

Shopping · · · · · · · · · · · · · · · · 12

Money, money · · · · · · · · · · · · 14

Flying high · · · · · · · · · · · · · · · 16

Follow that robot! · · · · · · · · · · 18

The future · · · · · · · · · · · · · · · 20

Extension activities · · · · · · · · · 22

Words to remember · · · · · · · · · 22

Activity answers · · · · · · · · · · · 23

Index · · · · · · · · · · · · · · · · · · · 24

Children will need access to the Internet for
most of the activities in this book. Parents
or teachers should supervise this and
discuss staying safe online with children.

# Getting started

Hi! I'm Data Duck. I'm going to tell you about the computers that are all around us. We can't always see them, but they play a big part in our lives every day.

All around us, there are computers that control machines, vehicles, robots, lights and many other things. They can do this because of the way they are programmed. When we program a computer, we tell it what to do using code.

**DATA DUCK**
Code is a set of instructions we use to tell computers what to do. In this book, we will be using coding blocks, like the one below. Coding blocks are instructions that we can combine to create code for a computer.

Change height by -10 m

Play duck call

There are lots of activities in the book for you to try out. There are also some online activities for you to practise. For the online activities, go to **www.blueshiftcoding.com/kidsgetcoding** and look for the activity with the page number from the book.

# Everyday computers

Did you know that computers aren't just in our homes and schools? They are around us almost all the time. Computers control the street lights, our cars and things such as lights and alarms in and around our homes.

Many of these computers around us include something called a 'sensor'. Sensors can pick up on certain things around them. Some can measure the temperature, others whether it is light or dark, and some can sense if there are any objects nearby.

**Street lights:** A street light uses a light sensor to find out when it's getting dark. Once night-time falls, its light turns on.

**House:** Some houses have a motion sensor outside. It can find out if somebody is moving towards the house at night, and turn on a light.

**Car:** Some cars have distance sensors. These sensors can find out how far away the car is from other objects, such as a wall. Drivers use these sensors when they are parking their car.

{4}

## Lights on!

Some cars turn on their headlights when it gets dark outside.
Can you work out which kind of sensor a car uses to do this?
A. A sensor that measures the distance between itself and the car in front.
B. A sensor that measures how light or dark it is outside.
C. A sensor that measures the temperature outside.

Turn to page 23 to see the answers.

**DATA DUCK**
Sensors are a bit like our senses! Do you remember what our senses are? Think of three senses and what they can do.

# Car or computer?

Cars have many computers in them – some even have hundreds! These computers, or processors, all make sure the car works the way it should.

There are computers that control the car's heating, its speed and its lights. Some computers can show maps of the area the car is in, while others can play music. Some cars have so many clever computers that they can even drive themselves!

**DATA DUCK**

In a car, the sensors pass on the information they find out to the car's computer. This is called input. Then, the computer passes on signals to other parts of the car to tell it to do certain things. This is called output.

## Time for a refill

Drivers need to know in good time when their car's petrol tank needs refilling, because they still need to be able to drive to the petrol station. Look at the inputs and outputs below, and pick which ones mean this car's computer is doing its job properly.

Turn to page 23 to see the answers.

**Input:**

1. Tank sensor tells computer tank is full.

2. Tank sensor tells computer tank is empty.

3. Tank sensor tells computer tank is nearly empty.

**Output:**

1. Computer passes on signal to warning light: start flashing.

2. Computer passes on signal to radio: play music.

3. Computer passes on signal to heating: switch on.

# Road safety

Traffic lights are very important. They keep people who are crossing the street safe. They also keep traffic moving, so that we can all get to where we need to go. And they all work with sensors!

Traffic light sensors can detect when there is a lot of traffic or when someone is waiting to cross the street. The sensors pass this information on to the computer. The computer then sends on a signal to the lights, so they change to red, amber or green at the right time.

**DATA DUCK**
It's very important for the traffic light's computer, or processor, to change the lights at the right time. This helps everyone on the road stay safe.

## Change the lights

Traffic light computers are programmed to make sure they pass on the right information to the lights. Have a look at the information below, and choose which signals the computer needs to send to the lights.

Turn to page 23 to see the answers.

**Sensor information:** There are many people waiting to cross the road.

**Computer signal to lights:**

A: Turn red for cars. Then turn green for people, so they can cross.

B: Remain green for cars. Turn green for people, too.

**Sensor information:** There are many cars waiting at a red light, and not many people (pedestrians) crossing the road.

**Computer signal to lights:**

A: First, turn green for cars. Then, turn red for pedestrians.

B: First, turn red for pedestrians. Then, turn green for cars.

# Home sweet home

Computers in our home help keep us safe and comfortable. They make sure our rooms aren't too cold, they tell us when there is a fire and they switch on lights when it's dark outside.

**Alarm system:** Sensors tell a computer when a door or a window is opened. The computer sends a signal to switch on a loud alarm. Some computers even send a signal to the police, so they know there has been a break-in.

**Smoke detector:** Sensors tell a computer when there is smoke in the house. The computer sets off an alarm to warn people that something is burning.

**Automatic light:** A movement sensor tells a computer when someone is moving outside the house. The computer switches on the outside light.

**Thermostat:** This computer uses a temperature sensor to check whether rooms are too cold or warm. The computer then passes on the right signal to the heating system.

## Invent it!

Can you think of a computer you would like to invent for your house? What would it be able to do? Can you think of the sorts of sensors it might use? Draw your invention and explain how it would work.

## DATA DUCK

There are many other great inventions that can help around the home: mini robots that vacuum the floor in any room when it gets dirty, and devices that make sure plants get watered at the right time. All of these inventions use computers!

# Shopping

When we go to a shop, computers keep track of what we buy and how much we pay. Most of the time, the computers find out all this information thanks to something called a 'barcode'.

A barcode is a picture made up of lots of lines and numbers. You can find a barcode on the back of this book! Computers can read barcodes with the help of a sensor called a scanner. The barcodes help computers to find out what the scanned item is and how much it costs.

## DATA DUCK

At a shop check-out till, all the items a customer would like to buy are scanned. The information on the barcode is passed on from the scanner to the till's computer. The computer then adds up the cost of all the items and shows the amount on the till screen.

## Time to add up

Imagine you are the till's computer. Which total amount would you send to the screen of the till if the scanner passed on this information:

Turn to page 23 to see the answers.

| cheese | £2 |
|--------|----|
| fish   | £3 |
| milk   | £1 |
| bread  | £1 |
|        |    |

# Money, money

At shop tills, we use scanners and computers to tell us how much we need to pay for our shopping. And when we pay, we sometimes use even more computers!

People can pay for things by using a bank card or even their phone. They do this by tapping the phone or the card on a small machine, called a reader. During the tap, information is sent to and from the reader so that money goes from the person's bank account to pay the shop.

**DATA DUCK**
All computers need a battery (or electricity) to work. So the reader sends electric power to the bank card. This means that the card is powered and can now send and receive information.

# Tap to pay

Data Duck is at the shop and wants to buy some eggs that cost £1.50. He taps his card on the reader, but gets an error message and a beep. He can't pay with his card. What might have happened?

A. He only has £1 left in his bank account.

B. The machine can't connect to the bank.

C. His card is cracked.

D. Any of the above.

Turn to page 23 to see the answers.

# Flying high

Planes, helicopters and even small flying robots, called drones, all need sensors and computers to fly. Without them, these aircraft wouldn't even be able to lift off the ground.

One of the most important sensors is the distance sensor, which can measure the distance between the aircraft and the ground. The pilot needs to know this information so that she can make sure the aircraft doesn't land too soon, or crash.

## DATA DUCK

Aircraft sensors send their information to a processor (computer). The processor then passes the information on to the dashboard, where the pilot can read it.

### Keep it up!

Look at the coding blocks below, and choose which one needs to sit in the gap so the drone never flies too high.

Turn to page 23 to see the answers.

If height over 100 m then

Repeat until height under 100 m

Play duck call

Change height by -10 m

Turn to left

# Follow that robot!

Robots are used for many things, from building cars to moving goods. Inside the robot, a computer is connected to sensors and motors. The motors make the robot move.

One kind of robot that uses sensors and motors to move around is called a line-following robot. It can follow a line on the ground. This is because there is a sensor at the bottom of the robot that can find out where the line is. The computer makes sure the robot follows the line as it moves around.

**DATA DUCK**
We can program the computers inside these robots to do all sorts of amazing things. There are robots that can help doctors perform operations. Others can build cars or even play table tennis!

## Build a robot!

Let's build our own robot! To help it work, we need to make sure our robot has an input, a processor and an output. Look at the list below and pick one of each. What will your robot be able to do?

**Input:**

1. Distance sensor – this can find out how far away objects are from the robot

2. Light sensor – this can find out whether it is light or dark around the robot

**Output:**

1. Motor attached to arms – this means our robot can do things such as flick a light switch

2. Motor attached to wheels – this means our robot can move around

# The future

Computers are everywhere. They can be so tiny that we can barely see them. They can send information to each other and to devices, such as phones, without needing any wires.

We can now wear computers, for example smart watches. These are watches with tiny computers in them that tell us things about ourselves. They can show us how fast we are breathing, and how long we slept last night.

## DATA DUCK

We can put computers inside the machines we use every day, such as kettles and toasters! These machines can send and receive information from other computers. For example, we could use a phone to switch on the kettle!

## A toast to friends!

Someone has invented a toaster that sends a message to all your friends when you make a piece of toast! Now it's your turn. Think about what your toaster of the future might be able to do. Write down or draw your design.

# Extension activities

Go to **blueshiftcoding.com/kidsgetcoding** for more fun activities and to practise:

- using coding blocks
- writing programs
- predicting what programs will do
- exploring sensors

# Words to remember

**code**        the arrangement of instructions in a computer program.

**dashboard**   in cars and planes, a panel with controls and information that is fitted in front of the driver or pilot.

**input**       something that puts information into a computer, such as a sensor.

**output**      something used to send information out of a computer, such as a warning light or an alarm.

**scanner**     a device that is used to 'read' barcodes and send the information to a computer.

**sensor**      a device that works like our senses, and can measure light, temperature, movement and other things.

# Activity answers

## p. 5

B. A sensor that measures how light or dark it is outside sends a signal to the car's computer to turn on the headlights when it's dark.

## p. 7

Input:

3. Tank sensor tells computer tank is nearly empty.

Output:

1. Computer passes on signal to warning light: start flashing.

## p. 9

Sensor information: There are many people waiting to cross the road.

Computer signal to lights:

A: Turn red for cars. Then turn green for people, so they can cross.

Sensor information: There are many cars waiting at a red light, and not many people (pedestrians) crossing the road.

Computer signal to lights:

B: First, turn red for pedestrians. Then, turn green for cars.

## p. 13

The computer would send the amount of £7 to the till's screen (£2 + £3 + £1 + £1 = £7).

## p. 15

D. Any of the above.

## p. 17

> If height over 100 m then
>
> > Repeat until height under 100 m
> >
> > > Change height by -10 m

# Index

aircraft 16, 17

car 4, 5, 6–7, 18

code 3

computer 3, 4, 6–7, 8, 9, 10, 11, 12, 13, 14, 17, 18, 20, 21

home 4, 10–11

processor 6, 9, 17, 19

sensor 4, 5, 6, 7, 8, 9, 10, 11, 12, 16, 17, 18, 19

robot 3, 11, 16, 18–19

First published in Great Britain in 2017 by Wayland

Copyright © Hodder & Stoughton Ltd, 2017

Text copyright © Heather Lyons, 2017

Editor: Liza Miller
Cover illustrator: Alex Westgate
Illustrator: Dan Crisp
Freelance editor: Julia Adams
Designer: Tim Mayer (Mayer Media)

ISBN: 978 1 5263 0222 9
10 9 8 7 6 5 4 3 2 1

MIX
Paper from
responsible sources
FSC® C104740
FSC
www.fsc.org

Wayland
An imprint of
Hachette Children's Group
Part of Hodder & Stoughton
Carmelite House
50 Victoria Embankment
London EC4Y 0DZ

An Hachette UK Company
www.hachette.co.uk
www.hachettechildrens.co.uk

Printed in China